GW00578034

PETER ILYITCH TCHAIKOVSKY

Romeo and Juliet Overture
and
Capriccio Italien

in Full Score

DOVER PUBLICATIONS, INC., NEW YORK

Copyright © 1986 by Dover Publications, Inc.
All rights reserved under Pan American and International
Copyright Conventions.

This Dover edition, first published in 1986, is an unabridged
republication, in a single volume, of two works from the set
P. Čaĭkovskiĭ, Polnoe sobranie sočineniĭ (Complete Works),
published by the Gosudarstvennoe Muzykal'noe Izdatel'stvo
(State Music Publishing House), Moscow and Leningrad. The
Romeo and Juliet Overture (third, definitive version) is from Vol.
23 (1950), edited by Anatoliĭ Drozdov and Igor' Belz. Capriccio
Italien is from Vol. 25 (1961), edited by A. A. Nikolaev. Both
volumes fall within the subcategory Sočineniya dlya orkestra
(Orchestral Works).

The table of contents and main headings have been prepared,
and the original Russian editorial remarks and footnotes newly
translated into English, by Stanley Appelbaum specially for the
present edition. The musical errata in Romeo and Juliet listed in
the Russian volume have been tacitly corrected here.

The publisher is grateful to Queens College (Aaron Copland
School of Music and Paul Klapper Library) for making the music
available for direct photographing.

Manufactured in the United States of America
Dover Publications, Inc., 31 East 2nd Street,
Mineola, N.Y. 11501

Library of Congress Cataloging-in-Publication Data

Tchaikovsky, Peter Ilich, 1840–1893.
[Romeo et Juliette (Fantasy-overture)]
Romeo and Juliet overture ; and, Capriccio italien.

For orchestra.
Reprint. Originally published: Moscow :
Gosudarstvennoe muzykal'noe izdatel'stvo, 1950 (1st work) and
1961 (2nd).
1. Overtures—Scores.   2. Orchestral music—Scores.
I. Tchaikovsky, Peter Ilich; 1840–1893. Capriccio italien.
1986.   II. Title: Romeo and Juliet overture.
III. Title: Capriccio italien.
M1000.T4   1986   86-752595
ISBN 0-486-25217-5 (pbk.)

Contents

Note

In the Russian edition on which this Dover volume is based (see copyright page for bibliographic details), the editorial remarks on *Capriccio Italien* take the form of footnotes to the music pages. In the present volume, new English translations replace those Russian footnotes on the appropriate pages. For the *Romeo and Juliet Overture*, on the other hand, the Russian edition had a separate remarks section, a new English translation of which now follows:

Mm. 4–5, Cl., Fg.: The autograph MS lacks the ◁ and the "poco più f."

M. 81, Fl.: Thus in all editions; in the MS this note is given to the first flute only.

M. 234, Vle: In the MS, this measure is an exact repetition of the preceding one.

M. 290, Trb. I: In the [four-hand piano] arrangement by N. N. Purgol'd [published in Tchaikovsky's lifetime], the top note of the chord in the first quarter is not *e♭* but *e*, and in the analogous measure 312 it is not *e* but *e♯*.

M. 300, Cl.: Thus in all editions; the MS has:

M. 328, Archi: The MS lacks the indication, "molto."

M. 332, Fl.: The MS has

Mm. 337–338, C. i.: The MS has

This is obviously a slip of the pen (the octave doubling of the bass in the middle voice is undesirable), which the composer corrected in the proof stage.

M. 338, Picc., Fl., Ob., Cl., Fg., Cr., Trbn., Tb.: In the second half of the measure, for all winds, the MS has two quarter-notes (instead of syncopated eighths).

M. 339, Cr. III, IV: In the Ms, the last quarter is

clearly a slip of the pen, which the composer corrected in proof.

M. 353, Cl.: For the second quarter, the MS has

M. 364, Tp., G. c.: The MS has quarter-notes (without syncopation).

M. 367, V. II, Vle, Vc., Cb.: The MS has eighths, not sixteenths.

M. 371, Ob., Cl.: The MS lacks the indication "espressivo."

Mm. 381–382, Cr. I: The MS lacks the tie between these two measures.

M. 384, V. I, II: Thus in the MS and the four-hand arrangement by N. N. Purgol'd. In the printed scores and instrumental parts, the first quarter in the second violins and the third quarter in the first violins is

M. 390, Archi: In the MS, all the bowed strings except the Cb. have the indication "largamente."

M. 401, Fl. II: In the MS, the first quarter is *b*; in the printed scores, *g*.

M. 405, Fl. II: In the MS, the first quarter is *c♯*; in the printed scores, *a* (by analogy with m. 401).

M. 409, Fg. I: In the printed score, the second half-note is *g♮*.

Mm. 411–413, Trb. I: The MS has the obvious error

M. 413, Trbn. III: The MS has

M. 417, C. i.: Thus in the printed scores; the MS has

an obvious error corrected by the composer in proof.

M. 419, Cl.: The MS has [notation] , an obvious error corrected by the composer in proof.

M. 435, Archi: In the MS, for all the bowed strings except the Cb., near the last notes of this measure there are sharps (before the *a*'s), which were obviously discarded by the composer in proof.

Mm. 450–451, Fl. I, II: In the MS, the second half of m. 450 and all of m. 451 (except for the last sixteenth) are placed an octave lower in the second flute part, and the last note (*b*) of m. 451 is written an octave higher in the first flute part.

M. 453, Ob.: The MS has a quarter-note here, not an eighth.

Romeo and Juliet Overture

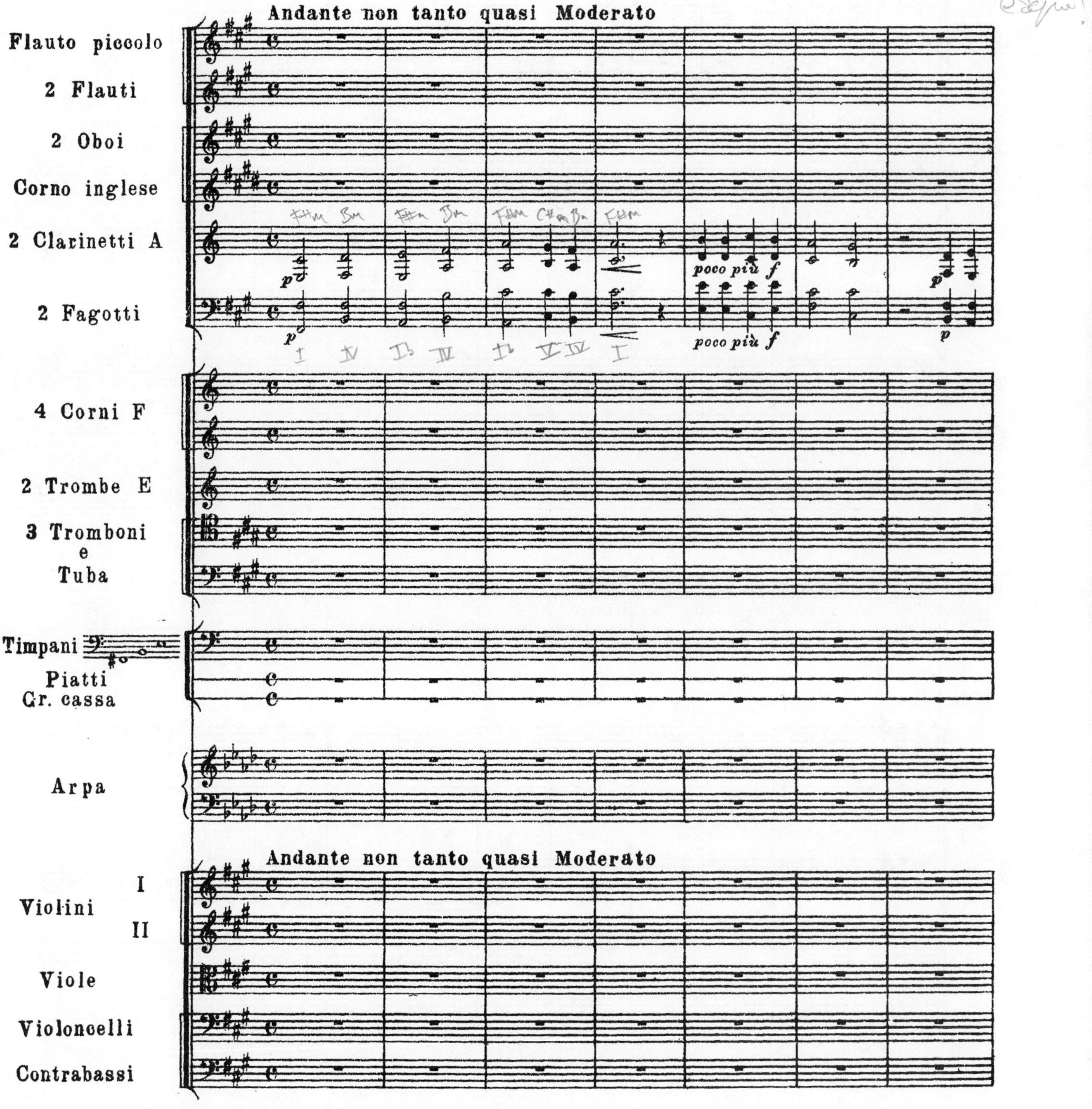

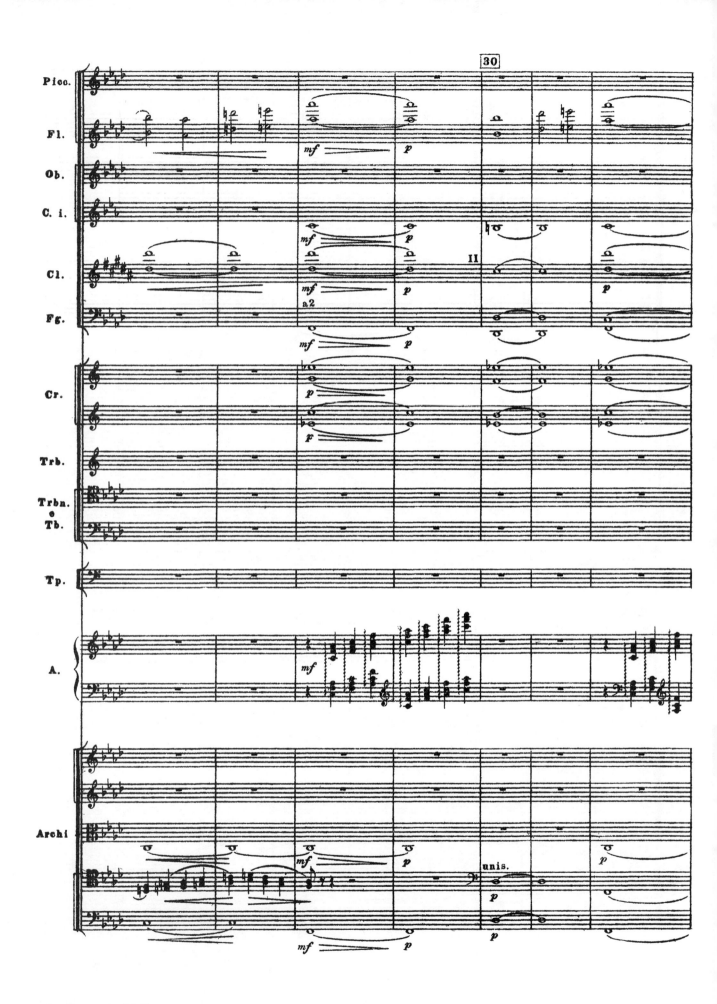

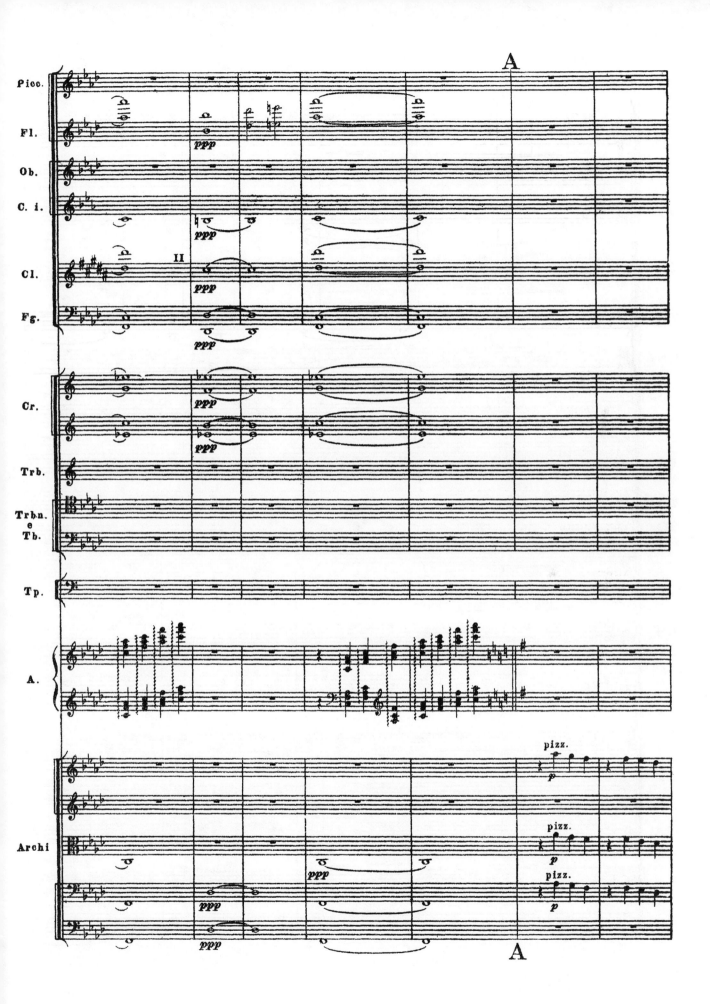

lots of rising and falling – trad. love theme!

Lots of added notes and suspensions

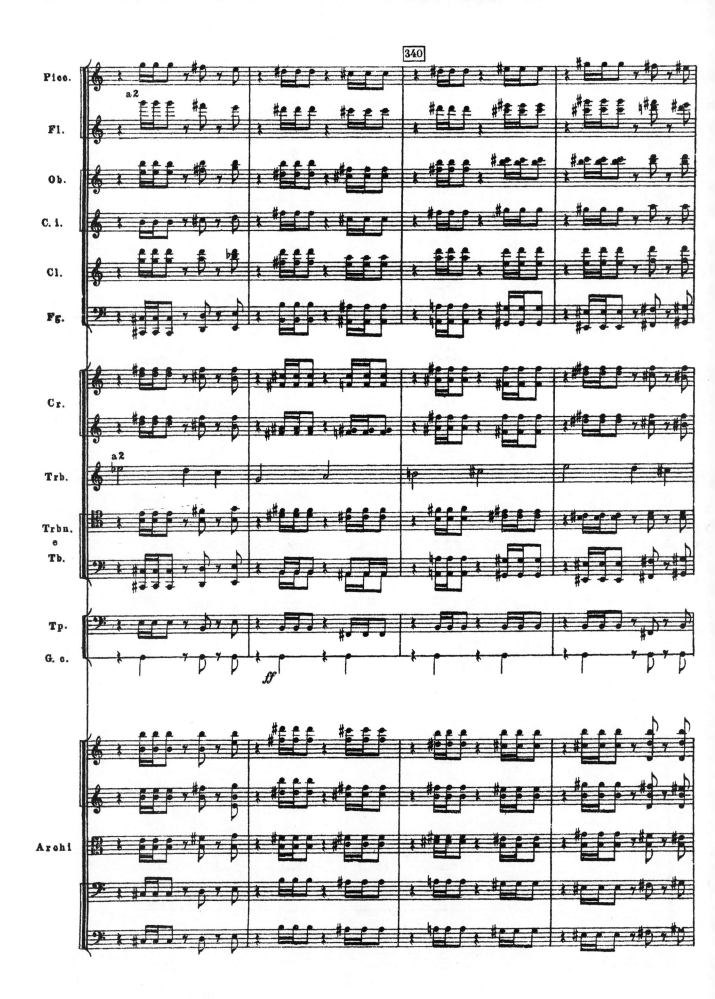

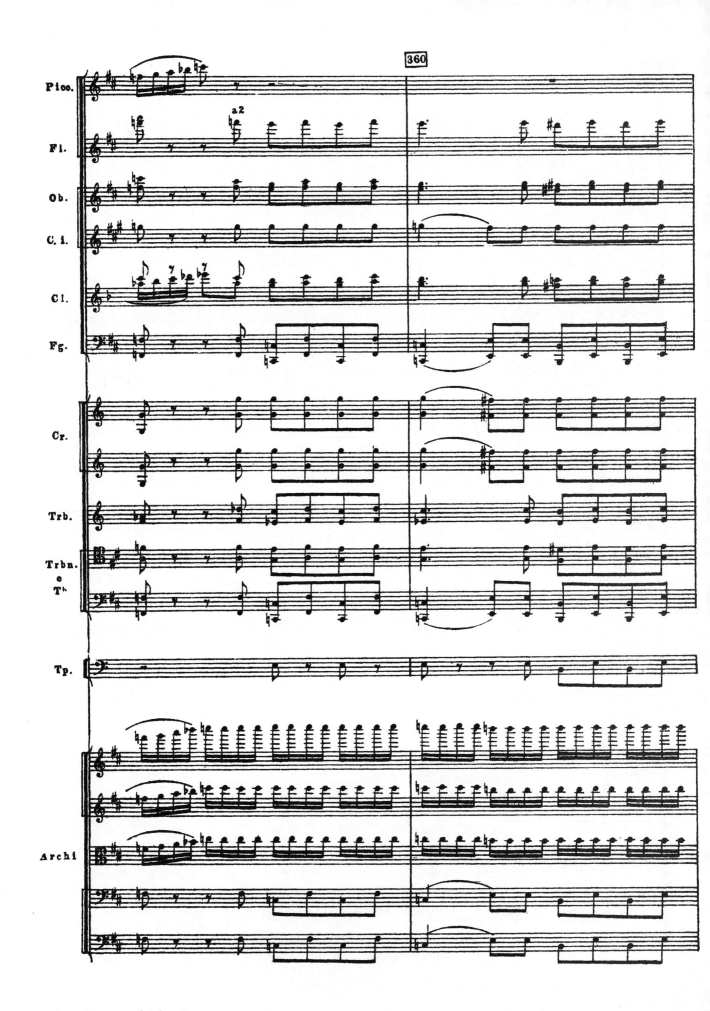

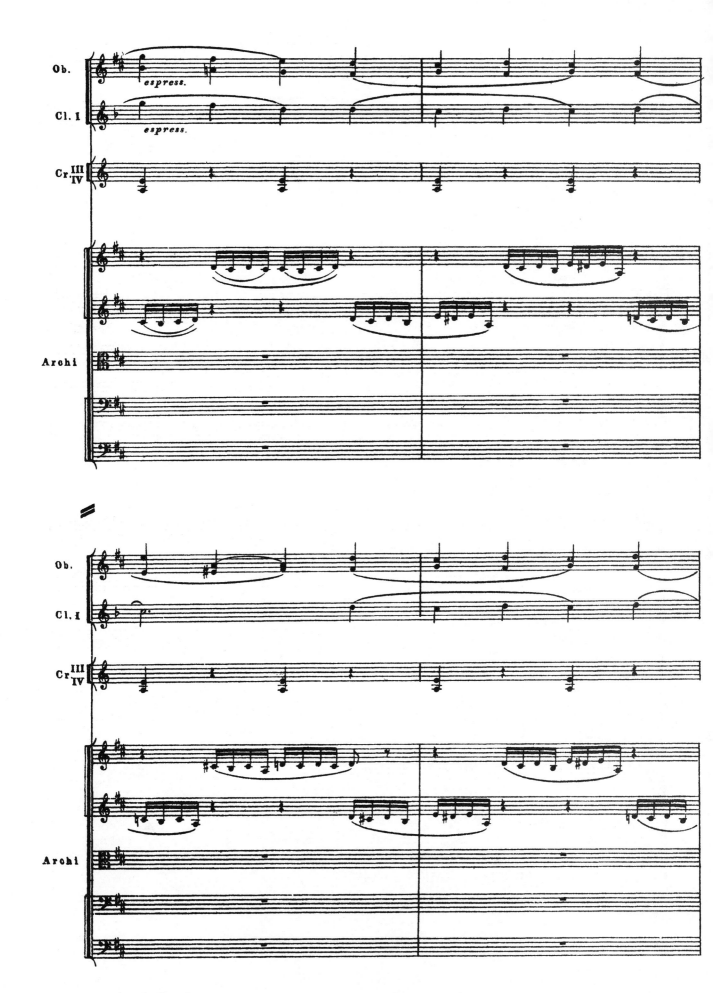

Romeo and Juliet Overture 77

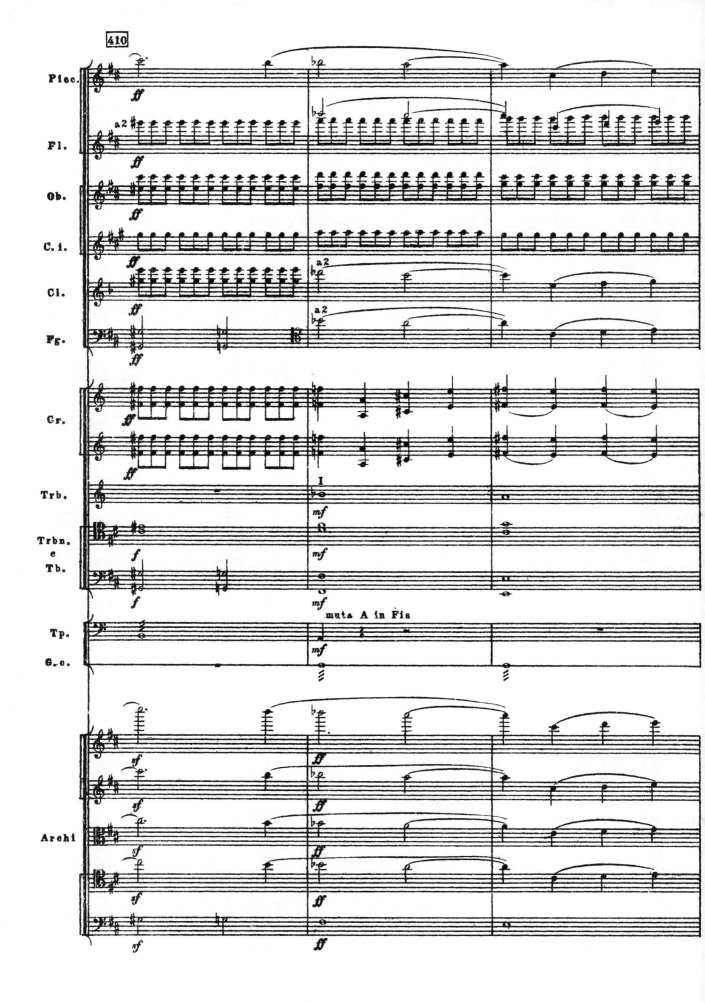

Capriccio Italien, Op. 45

1) In the autograph MS, these notes are assigned to the first cornet. The present text follows the Jürgenson edition [first edition, Moscow, 1880].

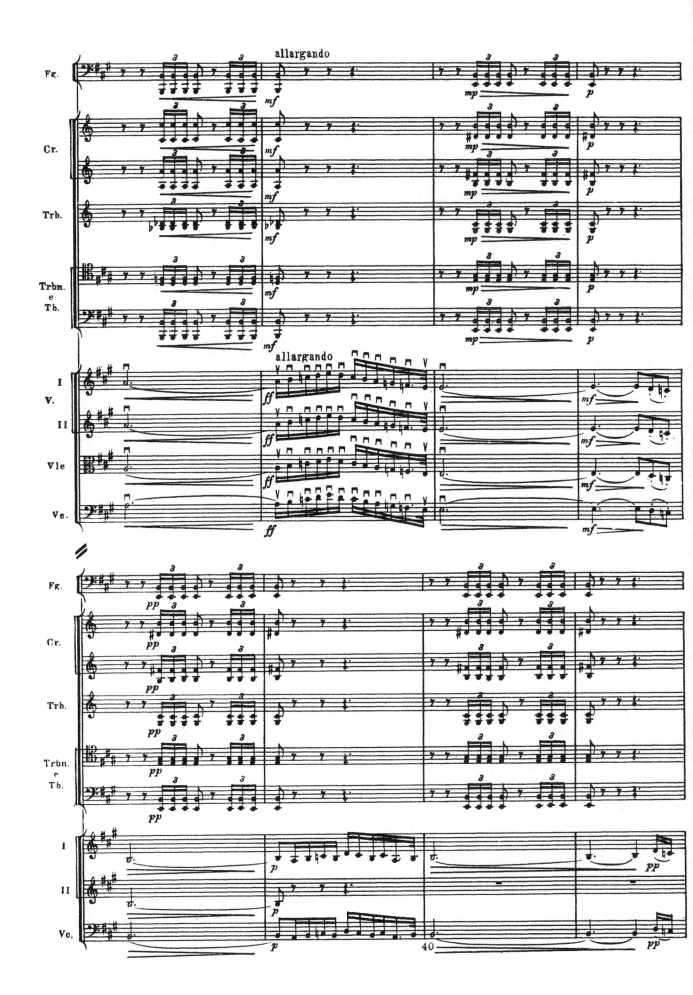

1) In the autograph MS, m. 69 in the cymbals part reads: ⊢——•——⊣ . The present text follows the Jürgenson edition.

1) In the autograph MS, m. 132 in the second violin part reads: [musical notation]. The present text follows the Jürgenson edition.

2) In the Jürgenson edition, m. 132 in the second violin part reads: [musical notation]. The present text follows the autograph MS.

1) In the autograph MS, m. 141 in the trumpet part is assigned to the second trumpet. The present text follows the Jürgenson edition.

1) In the autograph MS, the trombones and tuba are marked "mf."

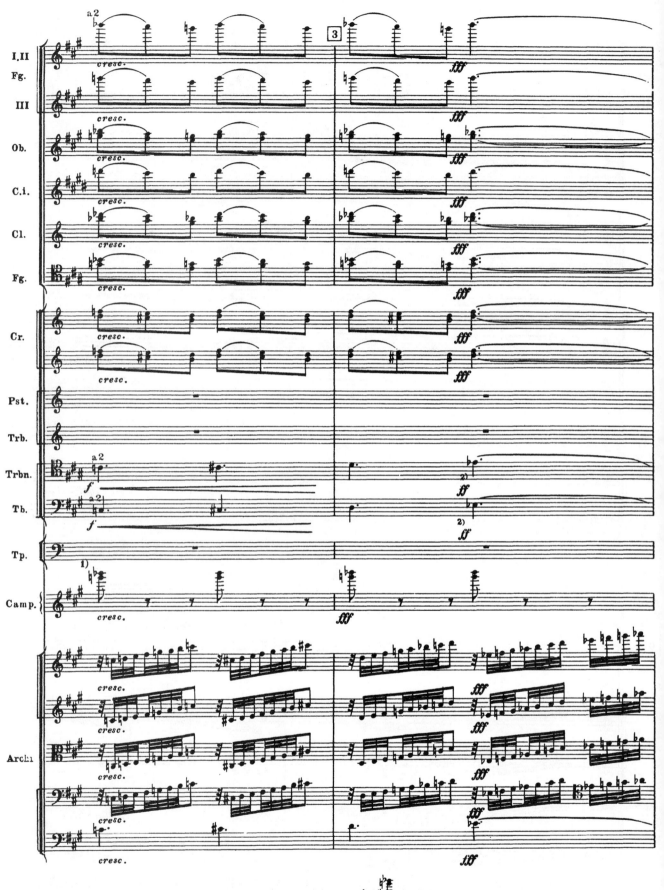

1) In the Jürgenson edition, m. 171 in the glockenspiel part reads: . The present text follows the autograph MS.

2) In the Jürgenson edition, in m. 172 the trombones and tuba are marked "fff." The present text follows the autograph MS.

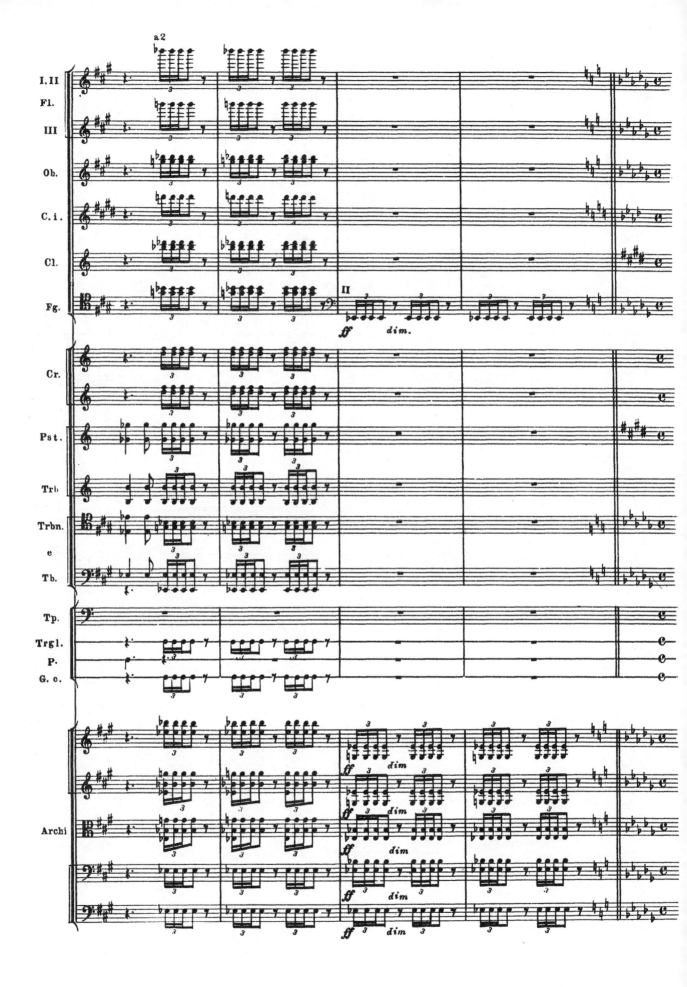

1) The Jürgenson edition lacks the first horn's accents in mm. 184, 186 and 188. The present text follows the autograph MS.

1) The Jürgenson edition lacks the first violins' accent in m. 189. The present text follows the autograph MS.

210

1) In the Jürgenson edition, m. 302 in the cornet part reads: [musical example]. The present text follows the autograph MS.

In m. 355 of the Jürgenson edition, the first and second violins lack the slurs between the third and fourth eighth-notes. The present text follows the autograph MS.

1) In m. 391, the autograph MS gives the trumpets , which is corrected in pencil to read: . This same

sixth occurs in the Jürgenson edition. The same holds for mm. 399 and 407.

1) In the Jürgenson edition, m. 419 in the clarinet part reads: . The present text follows the autograph MS.

1) In the autograph MS, m. 422 for horns I and II reads: [musical example] . The present text follows the Jürgenson edition.

2) In m. 424, in the first violin, second violin, viola and cello parts, the Jürgenson edition lacks the slurs. The same holds for m. 428. The present edition follows the autograph MS.

1) In the autograph MS, mm. 423–431, which are an exact repetition of mm. 409–417, are not written out but merely indicated by numbers. In the Jürgenson edition, in mm. 427 and 429 the harp part is omitted. It is restored here by analogy with mm. 414 and 416.

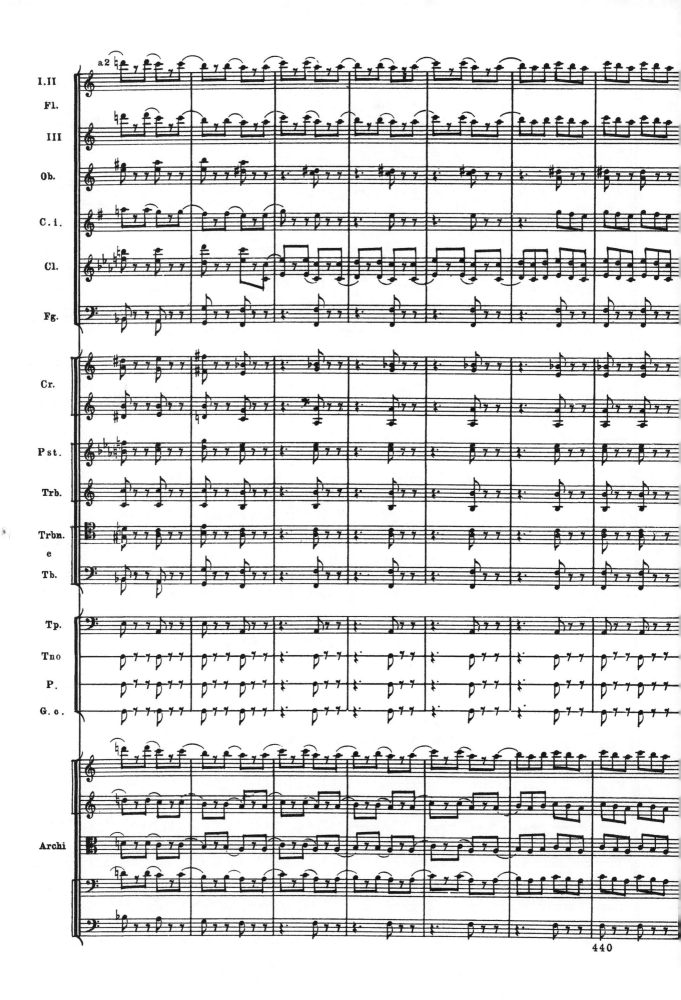

440

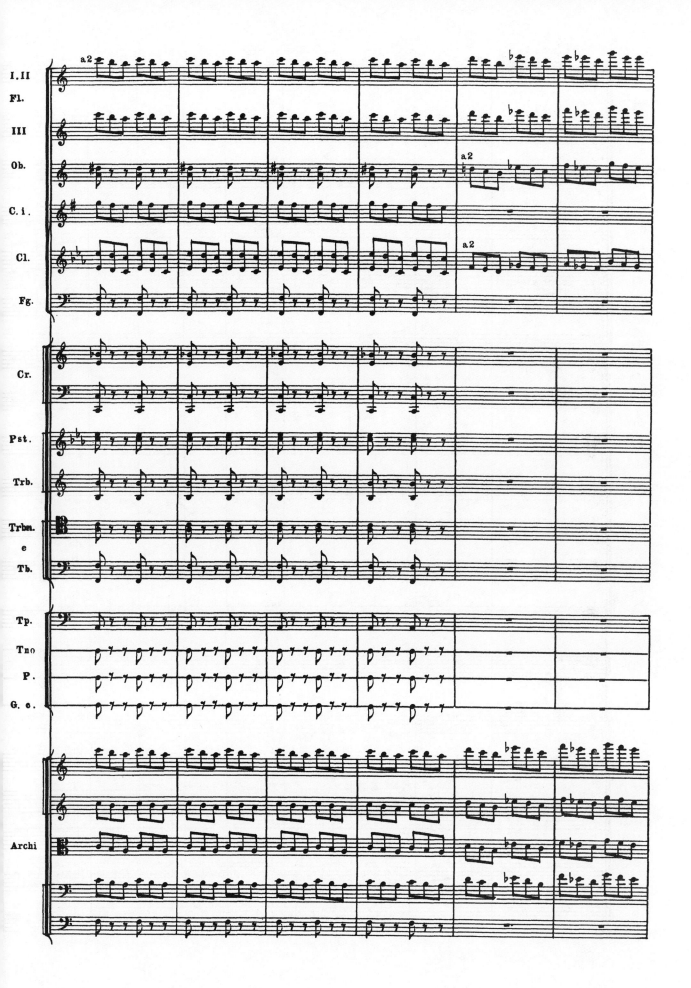

1) In m. 455, the autograph MS has the remark "Cassa sola."

1) In m. 475, the autograph MS gives the violas: ![notation] . The present text follows the Jürgenson edition.

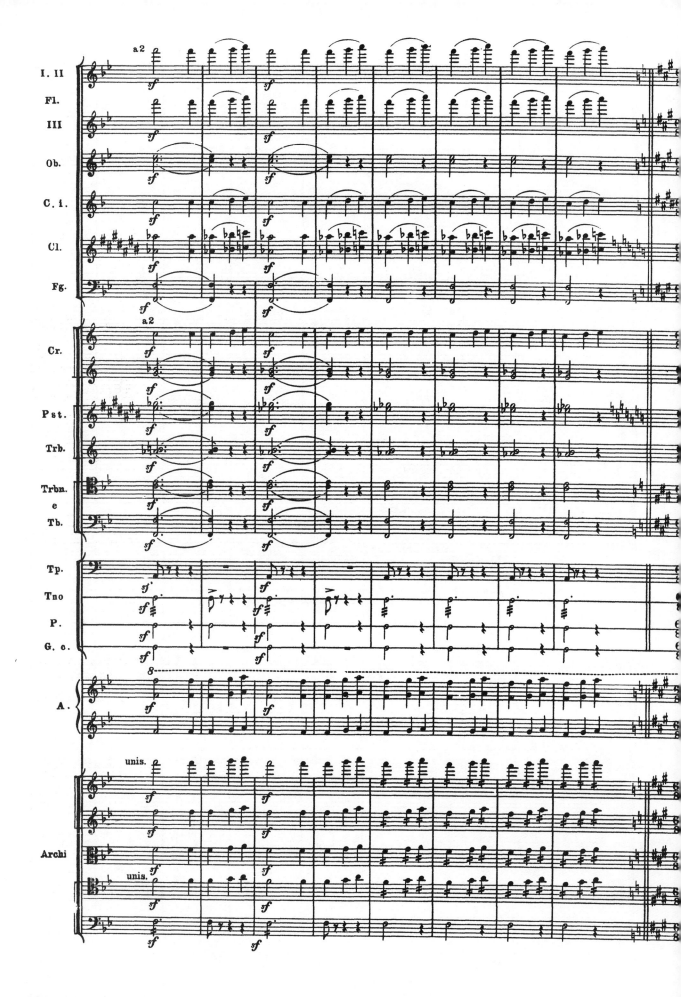

1) In m. 499, timpani part, the autograph MS has the indication "ffff," lacking in the Jürgenson edition.

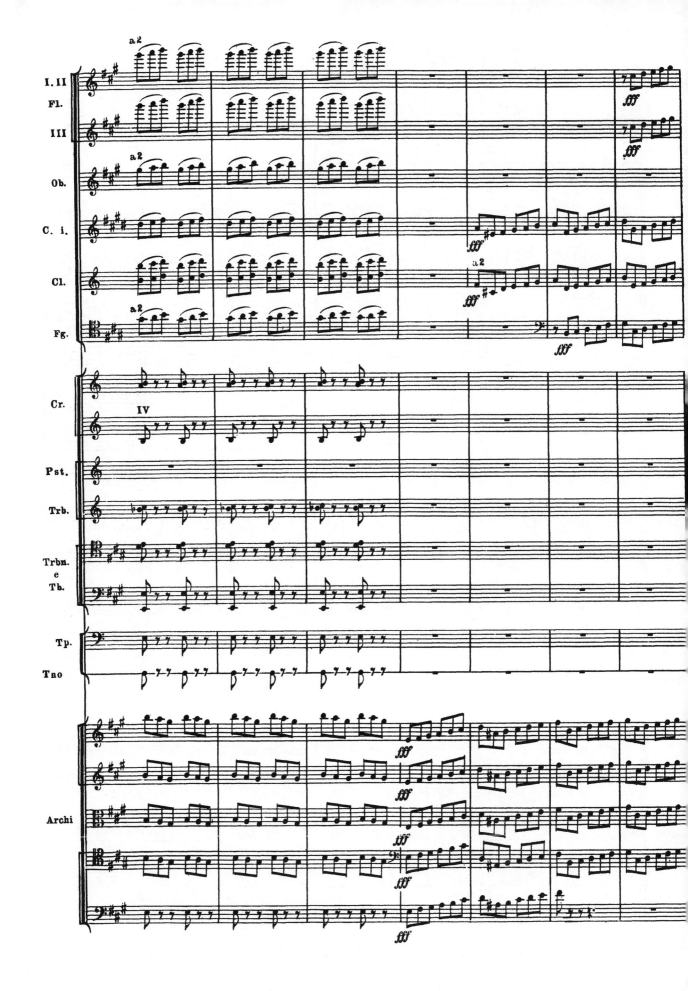

1) In m. 549, the autograph MS gives the trombones: ♭ 𝄞 . The present text follows the Jürgenson edition.

196   *Capriccio Italien*

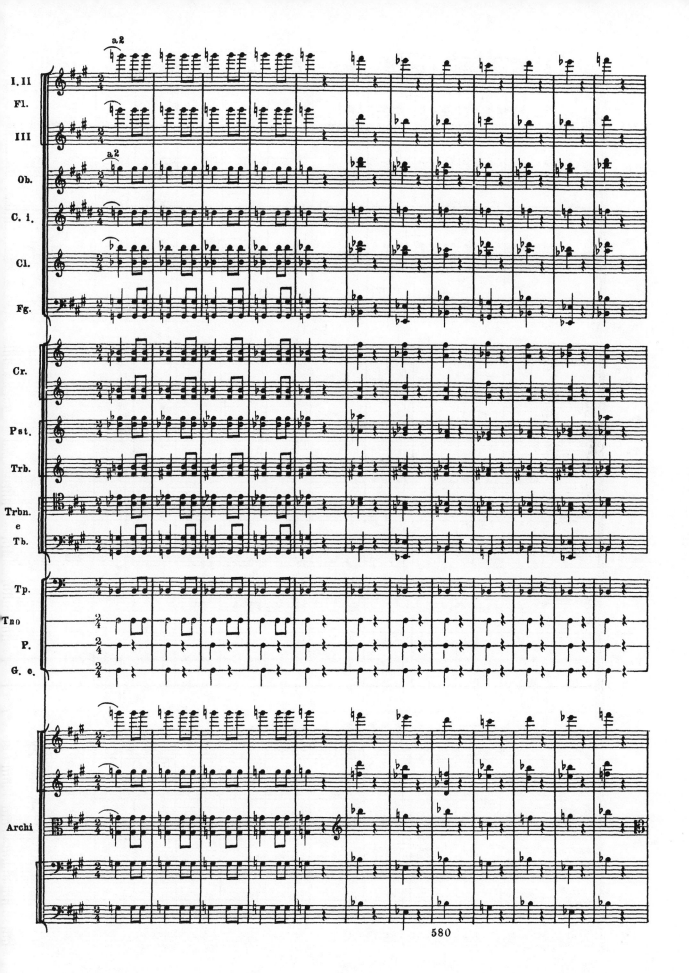

580

1) In the autograph MS, m. 590, the third flute has:

610

1) In m. 628, the autograph MS has the remark "P. soli."
2) In m. 629, the autograph MS has the remark "C. sola."
3) In the Jürgenson edition, m. 633 in the first and second violin parts reads: The present text follows the autograph MS.